# YOU CAN LISTEN TO DIRECTIONS

## STOP OR GO?

You Choose the Ending

by Connie Colwell Miller • illustrated by Victoria Assanelli

Do you ever wish you could change a story or choose a different ending?

## IN THESE BOOKS, YOU CAN!

Read along and when you see this:

WHAT HAPPENS NEXT?

Skip to the page for that choice, and see what happens.

Will Eric listen to his dad? Will he stop or go? Help Eric make choices by reading this book.

Eric, Kate, and their dad go to the mall. Kate needs new shoes. Eric is excited. If he follows directions, he will get a new toy. Dad says, "Eric, please wait here while I get your sister."

## WHAT HAPPENS NEXT?

→ If Eric runs ahead, turn the page.
If Eric waits for his dad, turn to page 20. ←

Eric is so excited that he runs ahead. Dad calls after him. "Eric, stop! Wait for me! Cars could be coming!"

Dad catches up. But once they are inside the mall,
Eric sees a fun cart.

TURN THE PAGE →

Eric runs ahead again. "Eric!" Dad says. "Don't go ahead without me! Please stay near me so I can keep you safe."

"Dad, can I push Kate?" Eric asks. He really wants to race the cart. "No, you kept running ahead. Stay next to me." Dad says.

## WHAT HAPPENS NEXT?

→ If Eric pushes the cart anyway, turn the page.

If he stops and lets his dad push the cart, turn to page 18. ←

Eric takes the cart and pushes Kate fast!

Dad shouts. "Eric! Stop! Your sister is not buckled! She could fall out!"

Eric stops. Dad buckles Kate and takes the cart.

"Eric," Dad says. "I need you to listen and stay by the cart, so I know you're safe."

## WHAT HAPPENS NEXT?

→ If Eric ignores his dad, turn the page.
If he stops and listens, turn to page 14. ←

Eric sees the toy store ahead. Dad says, "Eric, we need to buy your sister's shoes first. Do not go into the toy store." But Eric doesn't listen. He runs into the toy store.

TURN THE PAGE →

"Eric, where are you?"
Dad calls.

Finally, Dad finds Eric at the back of the toy store.

"Eric, I thought you were lost! We are going home now. You will not get a toy."

Eric is sad. If he had listened to his father, he would have earned a new toy.

THE END

Go to page 23.

Eric stops. He hadn't realized he wasn't listening well. He remembers that he might get a toy. So he tries to pay attention to his father's words.

"I'm sorry," Eric says.

TURN THE PAGE →

"I forgive you, Eric," says his dad, "but because you didn't listen today, you won't get a reward. There will be no toy."

Eric is disappointed. He should have followed his father's directions.

THE END

→ Go to page 23. ←

Sometimes listening is difficult for Eric. But then he remembers that he can get a toy if he follows directions. He looks at his dad and listens.

"Okay," Eric says. He moves to the side of the cart.

"Thank you," Dad says. "Following directions helps keep you safe, Eric."

Eric listens better on the rest of the shopping trip. Then, he gets to choose a new toy.

THE END

Go to page 23.

Eric follows his dad's directions. He waits near the trunk of the car. Dad takes Eric and Kate into the mall. They choose a fun cart. Eric gets to help push it.

 TURN THE PAGE →

After the shopping is done, Dad says, "Eric, you have been a great listener. Let's go to the toy store. You can pick out *two* new toys!"

THE END

- What choices did you make for Eric? How did that story end?
- What went well when Eric listened? What didn't work when Eric didn't listen?
- When is it important to stop and listen? When is it okay to go ahead?

We are all free to make choices, but choices have consequences. Would YOU listen to your parents, even if you didn't want to wait?

*With love for Mackenzie, who loves to go.—C.C.M.*

AMICUS ILLUSTRATED and AMICUS INK
are published by Amicus
P.O. Box 1329, Mankato, MN 56002
www.amicuspublishing.us

Library of Congress Cataloging-in-Publication Data
Names: Miller, Connie Colwell, 1976- author. | Assanelli, Victoria, 1984- illustrator.
Title: You can listen to directions : stop or go? / by Connie Colwell Miller ;
    illustrated by Victoria Assanelli.
Description: Mankato, Minnesota : Amicus, [2018] | Series: Making good choices
Identifiers: LCCN 2016057211 (print) | LCCN 2017009557 (ebook) |
    ISBN 9781681511665 (library binding) | ISBN 9781681512563 (ebook) |
    ISBN 9781681522357 (pbk.)
Subjects: LCSH: Listening—Juvenile literature. | Attention in children—Juvenile
    literature. | Decision making in children—Juvenile literature.
Classification: LCC BF323.L5 .M46 2018 (print) | LCC BF323.L5 (ebook) |
    DDC 155.4/19—dc23
LC record available at https://lccn.loc.gov/2016057211

Editor: Rebecca Glaser
Designer: Kathleen Petelinsek

Printed in North Mankato, Minnesota
HC 10 9 8 7 6 5 4 3
PB 10 9 8 7 6 5 4 3 2

## ABOUT THE AUTHOR

Connie Colwell Miller is a writer, editor, and instructor who lives in Mankato, Minnesota, with her four children. She has written over 80 books for young children. She likes to tell stories to her kids to teach them important life lessons.

## ABOUT THE ILLUSTRATOR

Victoria Assanelli was born during the autumn of 1984 in Buenos Aires, Argentina. She spent most of her childhood playing with her grandparents, reading books, and drawing doodles. She began working as an illustrator in 2007, and has illustrated several textbooks and storybooks since.